X GAMES

Skateboarding Big Air

GAMES

by Connie Colwell Miller

Reading Consultant:
Barbara J. Fox
Reading Specialist
North Carolina State University

Content Consultant:
Ben Hobson
Content Coordinator
Extreme Sports Channel
United Kingdom

Capstone
press

Mankato, Minnesota

Blazers is published by Capstone Press,
151 Good Counsel Drive, P.O. Box 669, Mankato, Minnesota 56002.
www.capstonepress.com

Library of Congress Cataloging-in-Publication Data
Miller, Connie Colwell, 1976–
   Skateboarding Big Air / by Connie Colwell Miller.
   p. cm.—(Blazers. X Games.)
   Includes bibliographical references and index.
   ISBN-13: 978-1-4296-0108-5 (hardcover)
   ISBN-10: 1-4296-0108-6 (hardcover)
   1. Skateboarding—Juvenile literature. 2. ESPN X-Games—Juvenile
literature. I. Title. II. Series.
GV859.8.M55 2008
796.22—dc22   2007001741

Summary: Describes the sport of skateboarding big air, focusing on the
   X Games, including competitions and star athletes.

Essential content terms are bold and are defined at the bottom of the page where they first appear.

Editorial Credits
Mandy R. Robbins, editor; Bobbi J. Wyss, designer; Jo Miller, photo researcher

Photo Credits
AP/Wide World Photos/Jae C. Hong, 13, 24; Ric Francis, cover (foreground),
   16–17, 25
Corbis/Icon SMI/Tony Donaldson, 20–21; NewSport/Matt A. Brown, 10–11;
   Osports.cn, 23; Steve Boyle, 4–5, 15
Shutterstock/Donald R. Swartz, cover (background); Taolmor, 18–19
stockxpert/huwbriscoe, 28–29; ronen, 14
ZUMA Press/K.C. Alfred/SDU-T, 6, 8; Quiksilver/DC, 26–27; Vaughn Youtz, 12

1 2 3 4 5 6 12 11 10 09 08 07

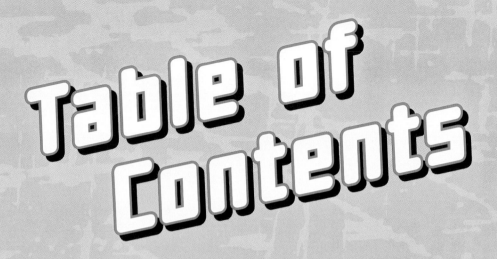

Table of Contents

Dropping Into the Ramp

In August 2006, the X Games were rocking in Los Angeles. Danny Way dropped into the **mega ramp**. He raced down the 80-foot (24-meter) ramp.

mega ramp (MEG-uh RAMP)—a ramp used in skateboarding big air; the mega ramp is nine stories high and about as long as a football field.

Way soared over a 70-foot (21-meter) gap in the mega ramp. While in the air he did a rocket air back flip. Way landed his board safely on the other side of the gap.

Then Way coasted up the **quarter pipe**. He exploded into another trick called an extended backside air.

quarter pipe (KWOR-tur PIPE)—a ramp that curves from being flat on the ground to pointing straight up

As Way landed, fans burst into cheers. This run earned Way his third gold medal in skateboarding big air.

Big Air Basics

Big air skaters take off down the mega ramp. Skaters speed down the 60-foot (18-meter) or the 80-foot (24-meter) roll-in.

roll-in (ROHL-IN)—a steep ramp skaters roll down to gain speed

Roll-ins help skaters speed toward large gaps in the ramp. Skaters do flips and other crazy tricks while sailing over the gaps.

BLAZER FACT

Skaters reach speeds close to 40 miles (64 kilometers) per hour on roll-ins.

Omar Hassan

Skaters try to land safely on the other side of the gap. Then they do another **aerial** off the 27-foot (8-meter) quarter pipe. Skaters mix twists, flips, and grabs during aerials.

aerial (AIR-ee-uhl)—a trick skaters perform while soaring through the air

Competing in Big Air

The X Games holds the only skateboarding big air competition. In the first round, eight skaters take four runs down the mega ramp.

Andy Macdonald

The best three skaters move on. They challenge the best three skaters from the last X Games. Judges rate skaters on style and jump height. Winners earn prizes worth thousands of dollars.

BLAZER FACT

Danny Way holds the record for the longest skateboard jump. It is 79 feet (24 meters)!

Mega Ramp Diagram

landing ramp

quarter pipe

gap

roll-ins

jumps

X GAMES

GAMES

SATURN

Mountain Dew

TACO BELL

RIGHT GUARD

SUPERCROSS

Big Air Records

Most fans agree that Danny Way is the best big air skater. He holds the record for the highest jump off a ramp. In 2003, he rocketed 23.5 feet (7.2 meters) in the air.

Danny Way

Great Wall
of China

Andy Macdonald

Some other big air stars are Andy Macdonald, Jake Brown, and Rob Lorifice. In 2005, 18-year-old Lorifice was the youngest big air competitor ever.

Jake Brown

In big air, skaters continue to push for higher jumps on the mega ramp. The popularity of the sport is sure to grow along with the size of the jumps.

Danny Way has dropped out of a helicopter and onto a ramp. He calls this move the bomb drop!

Catching Big Air!

Glossary

aerial (AIR-ee-uhl)—a trick that is done in the air

competition (kom-puh-TISH-uhn)—a contest between two or more people

mega ramp (MEG-uh RAMP)—a large ramp that has two roll-ins at one end, a large gap in the center, and a quarter pipe at the other end

quarter pipe (KWOR-tur PIPE)—a ramp that curves from being flat on the ground to pointing straight up

roll-in (ROHL-IN)—a steep ramp that skaters roll down to gain speed

Read More

Blomquist, Christopher. *Skateboarding in the X Games.* A Kid's Guide to the X Games. New York: PowerKids Press, 2003.

Higgins, Matt. *Insider's Guide to Action-Sports.* New York: Scholastic, 2006.

Loizos, Constance. *Skateboard!: Your Guide to Street, Vert, Downhill, and More.* Washington, D.C.: National Geographic, 2002.

Internet Sites

FactHound offers a safe, fun way to find Internet sites related to this book. All of the sites on FactHound have been researched by our staff.

Here's how:
1. Visit *www.facthound.com*
2. Choose your grade level.
3. Type in this special code **1429601086** for age-appropriate sites. You may also browse subjects by clicking on letters, or by clicking on pictures or words.
4. Click on the **Fetch It** button.

FactHound will fetch the best sites for you!

Index